DOYLE
Ó ꝺUBHGHAILL

IRISH FAMILY NAMES

DOYLE
Ó DUBHGHAILL

Dáithí Ó hÓgáin

GILL & MACMILLAN

Published In Ireland by
Gill & Macmillan Ltd
Hume Avenue, Park West
Dublin 12
with associated companies throughout the world
www.gillmacmillan.ie
Text © Salamander Books 2003
0 7171 3560 8

Published by arrangement with Salamander Books Ltd, London

A member of **Chrysalis** Books plc

A CIP catalogue record is available for this book from the British Library.

9 8 7 6 5 4 3 2 1

All correspondence concerning the content of this volume should be addressed to
Salamander Books Ltd.

THE AUTHOR
Dáithí Ó hÓgáin, MA, PhD, is Associate Professor at University College Dublin,
Ireland, where he lectures on Irish folklore. He is the author of over 20 books,
several of them in Irish, on aspects of folk culture, history and tradition. He is also
a noted poet and short-story writer, and is a well-known conference lecturer. He
has participated in the production of documentary films in Europe and the United
States, and is a frequent TV and radio broadcaster.

CREDITS
Project Manager: Stella Caldwell
Design: Q2A Solutions
Picture Research: Julie McMahon
Cover Design: Cara Hamilton
Colour reproduction: Anorax, UK
Printed and bound in Italy

Special thanks to Antony Shaw for his invaluable advice and generous assistance in
writing the section on modern members of the family.

CONTENTS

INTRODUCTION

THE HISTORY OF IRELAND IS

A GREAT DRAMA OF WAR,

INVASION, PLANTATION,

IMMIGRATION, EMIGRATION,

CONFLICT AND SOLIDARITY.

INTRODUCTION

Above: The entrance to the passage grave at Newgrange in County Meath is a fine example of Neolithic architecture.

People have been in Ireland for about 9,000 years but, for over two-thirds of that time, what they called themselves either as individuals or as groups is unknown. The Celticisation of Ireland had begun by the fifth century BC, and a few centuries later it was complete. This process must have involved the coming of some influential groups from Britain and perhaps from the Continental land-mass. The Irish language developed from the Celtic spoken by these, and all our earliest surviving system of naming—whether of people or of places—are in that language.

From references to the country in ancient Greek and Latin sources, and from the earliest written traditions of the Irish themselves, the names of important early population groups in the country can be postulated. Since the country was known to outsiders as Éveriu ('the land'), the fusion of indigenous peoples and early Celtic settlers was termed 'the land-dwellers' i.e. Éverini or 'Iverni'. Within these Iverni, the various groups had different names, most prominent being the Vinducati, Soborgii, Darinii and Uluti towards the north, the Ceuleni and Aucii on the east coast, the Gamarnates in the west, and the Autinii and Veldobri in the south.

A strong challenge to the Iverni soon presented

itself in the form of an amalgam of peoples in the broad area of the southern midlands, headed by a band of warriors belonging to the Brigantes of central Britain who had crossed the Irish Sea. The group became known as Leiquni ('casters'), a name which was reinterpreted as Lagini ('lance-men'). These Lagini seem to have coalesced at an early date with another group of incomers called Gaiso-lingi ('javelin-jumpers'), and together they extended their power over most of the south-eastern quarter of Ireland.

In the first century AD, new groups were arriving from Britain, escaping from the devastation caused by the Roman legions. These, such as the Dumnonii and Coriondi, joined with the Lagini, who began to threaten

Above: The Petrie Crown, an example of early Irish Celtic metalworking.

Left: Dún Eoghanachta, a massive ring fort on the island of Inishmore. Probably built in the fifth century, the fort takes it name from the Eoghanacht people who ruled most of Munster at this time.

Above: St. Patrick makes his way to the ritual centre of Tara some time in the fifth century.

the Ivernian kingdom of the north midlands. There are several indications that the prestigious ritual centre of Tara was seized from the Iverni by the Lagini in or about the second century. Meanwhile, in the south another group—with origins in south-west Britain or in Brittany—was building up a strong power-base. This was the Venii, who divided into two sections. One of these sections remained in the south, winning more and more territory from the Ivernian tribes there; while the other section moved northwards along the west bank of the Shannon and began to threaten the Lagini. By the early fifth century, they had crossed the Shannon and seized Tara from the Lagini, whom they pushed southwards beyond the river Boyne. Further migrations into Ireland were caused by the Roman campaigns against the north of Britain in the second and third centuries. The Celtic and Celticised peoples of that area were called Priteni ('painters'), which name was changed to Cruithni in Ireland. Reaching Ireland, these migrants settled in scattered groups in the north-east and on both sides of the Shannon.

From all of these groups are descended the Gaelic people of Ireland, with names developing into specifically Irish forms. For instance, the name of the country

Éveriu became Ériu and later still Éire, while the Iverni became Érainn. Strong groups among them kept their separate designations—especially the Uluti ('bearded men'), who became Ulaidh. For their part, the Lagini became Laighin, and the Cruithni became Cruithin. The Venii became Féni, with their southern section known as Eoghanacht and their northern section known as Connachta. This latter in time became the most powerful of all Irish septs, controlling the Boyne valley, as well as the large area west of the Shannon which still retains their name.

Ireland came to be considered as naturally divided into five parts, each part called a 'fifth' (cúige)—Ulaidh in the north; Connachta in the west; Midhe ('centre') comprising the north midland plain; Laighin in the south-east; and Mumhain ('the nurturing' i.e. domain of the land-goddess) in the south. Later in English these were known respectively as Ulster, Connacht, Meath, Leinster and Munster. Midhe as a provincial unit ceased to exist in the Middle Ages, and its territory is in fact part of the modern increased province of Leinster. This accounts for the four historic provinces of Ireland. In modern Irish, of course, the Irish people themselves are called Gaeil or Éireannaigh, and the inhabitants of the four provinces are called

Below: Dry stone cells constructed by monks on the island of Skellig Michael some time in the sixth century are perfectly preserved.

Above: A map of 1700 showing the Irish provinces of Ulster, Munster, Leinster and Connacht before the partition of Ireland.

respectively Ultaigh, Connachtaigh, Laighnigh and Muimhnigh.

Many Irish septs are still identifiable in the mediaeval period as descendants of the Érainn, Laighin, Connachta and Eoghanacht, and a lesser number of the Cruithin. These population groups had, however, developed into loose federations of kingdoms, ruled by strong extended families called *cineál* ('septs'), each of which had a traditional septal name. A leader was referred to by his own personal name, and for clarity he was described as son of his named father. These simple patronymics gave way in the tenth and 11th centuries to habitual surnames of the type we now have. The septal names gradually came to be identified more with the territories inhabited by the septs than with the septs themselves.

In the year 795, the first Norse raiders appeared off the Irish coast, and within a generation or two they had progressed from being raiders to forming settlements. They set up some kingdoms inland, but those established by them on the sea-ports were more enduring. Despite the ebb and flow of almost incessant war in opposition to, and in alliance with different Irish septs, they remained an important force, with the Norse language being spoken in their settlements for several centuries. A considerable number of Irish surnames derive from the Norsemen, either by direct descent or by the interchange of culture.

The Normans, far-out cousins of the Irish Norsemen, conquered Ireland in the late 12th century, bringing with them Welsh, English, French and Flemish supporters. Within a century or two English became the dominant language among these settlers, but many of the chief Norman families in Ireland became strongly Gaelicised. They introduced a system of dividing the country into baronies, generally giving these baronies the names of the old septal territories. A large number of Irish surnames are of Norman extraction.

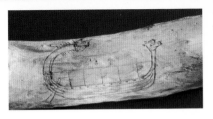

Above: Carving of a Norse ship.

The system of dividing Ireland into counties, each county comprising several baronies, dates from the reign of Queen Elizabeth I. Her successor, King James I, oversaw the Ulster Plantation, which brought in large numbers of settlers speaking Scottish Lallan, Scottish Gaelic and English. With the strengthening of rule from London, the English language gradually spread throughout the whole country and, with the widespread confiscation of land and its bestowal on settlers, many specifically English names entered the country. Most of these first names and some of the surnames developed Irish forms, but the contrary process was

Left: Norman ruins at sunset in Ballybunion, Co. Kerry.

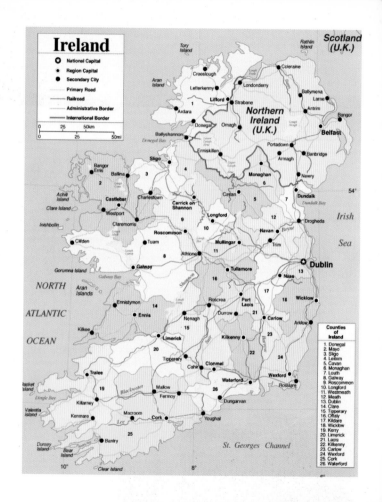

Ireland

- ✪ National Capital
- ● Region Capital
- ● Secondary City
- —— Primary Road
- —— Railroad
- —— Administrative Border
- —— International Border

0   25   50km
0   25   50mi

Counties of Ireland

1. Donegal
2. Mayo
3. Sligo
4. Leitrim
5. Cavan
6. Monaghan
7. Louth
8. Galway
9. Roscommon
10. Longford
11. Westmeath
12. Meath
13. Dublin
14. Clare
15. Tipperary
16. Offaly
17. Kildare
18. Wicklow
19. Kerry
20. Limerick
21. Laois
22. Kilkenny
23. Carlow
24. Wexford
25. Cork
26. Waterford

Scotland (U.K.)

Northern Ireland (U.K.)

Belfast

NORTH ATLANTIC OCEAN

Irish Sea

Dublin

St. Georges Channel

much stronger. Official versions of place-names were imposed in English, and anglicised forms of native Irish names were developed. It should be stressed that these anglicised forms, most prevalent in usage nowadays, are nearly all meaningless and give little indication of their derivation.

In Ireland there are numerous surnames of English, Scottish, Welsh, French, and other provenance. The histories of all these merit interest stretching beyond Ireland to their respective countries of origin. For general accounts of Irish surnames, see Edward MacLysaght, *Irish Families* (1957), *More Irish Families* (Dublin, 1960), *Supplement to Irish Families* (1964), and especially his *Surnames of Ireland* (1973). The last work contains a fine bibliography, as does Brian de Breffny, *Bibliography of Irish Family History and Genealogy* (1974). Further detail can be found in the many county and diocesan histories, as well as in learned journals which deal with historical and genealogical matters.

Argyle a muckle Scotch Knau in gude faith Sir.

Above: Satirical portrayal of Scottish Presbyterians who settled in Ulster during the 17th century.

Opposite page: A map of the modern counties of Ireland. The system of dividing Ireland into counties dates from the reign of Elizabeth I.

Left: A detail of the arms of the O'Malley family on the altar tomb in Clare Abbey.

GENEALOGY

IRELAND'S DRAMATIC

HISTORY, LIKE ALL HISTORY,

IS COMPOSED OF COUNTLESS

INDIVIDUAL FAMILY

HISTORIES, EACH UNIQUE.

GENEALOGY

As we have shown, the Irish—like other nationalities—are in reality a worthy mixture of many different peoples. Genealogy can give but a tiny insight into our background, for the available information tends to be uneven, focusing mostly on people of social standing. The study of genealogy is an enjoyable pastime, but it should not involve any exclusiveness, for our dignity depends not on our descent but on our common humanity and individual personalities.

The first step in researching one's genealogy is to talk to relatives and friends, particularly elderly ones, and to note down all the information they have about the family tree. This ought to trace the tree back through two generations at least.

Documents pertaining to the household can also be of help, no matter how ephemeral they may seem. A journey to the local library comes next to see if members of the family are mentioned in any documents or publications there. One can also consult inscriptions on graveyard headstones where family members are known to be buried. Lists of old gravestone inscriptions for many counties are kept in the Genealogical Office (GO) and the National Archives of Ireland, Dublin (NAI), and others are published in local journals.

Several parts of Ireland now have local heritage centres, in which copies and indexes of many records, as well as published works, are kept. Information in these centres will have been selected from the range of

Above: Tracing your family tree is an enjoyable pastime. The first step is to talk to elderly relatives and friends, and note down any information they can offer.
Previous pages: The Book of the Boyles, showing the descent of the earls of Cork and Orrery.

surviving sources for the study of Irish genealogy, and are listed here in general chronological order.

Earliest in date are the septal pedigrees—compiled at various periods from the sixth century AD to the Middle Ages. The prehistoric origins in these pedigrees are partly fanciful, but otherwise they provide invaluable material. The texts have been assembled by Michael A. O'Brien in *Corpus Genealogiarum Hiberniae* (1962). Several mediaeval and post-mediaeval genealogies have been edited and compiled by John O'Donovan —for whose work see R. I. Best, *Bibliography of Irish Philology and of Printed Irish Literature*, vol. 1 (1913), 295. Traditional pedigrees of various Irish septs are also given in editions such as Toirdhealbhach Ó Raithbheartaigh, *Genealogical Tracts* (1932); and Tadhg Ó Donnchadha, *An Leabhar Muimhneach* (1940). An edition by Nollaig Ó Muraile is forthcoming of the *Book of Genealogies* compiled from old sources by the 17th-century scholar, Dubhaltach Mac Fir Bhisigh.

A large number of pedigrees, compiled since the 16th century, are in GO. For the early 17th century, the

Above: Consulting the inscriptions of gravestones where family members are known to be buried can be a fruitful exercise in drawing up the family tree.

Left: The reading room of the National Library of Ireland, Dublin.

Calendar of Irish Patent Rolls of James I (published by IMC in 1966) gives the names of persons to whom land was granted by that king. For 1612–13, there is a list of 'Undertakers' i.e. English and Scottish landlords who were granted land in the Ulster Plantation (published in *The Historical Manuscripts Commission Reports*, vol. 4). For 1630 and 1642, the Muster Rolls name large landlords in Ulster and able-bodied men on whom they could call to fight (copies are in the NLI and the Public Record Office of Northern Ireland, Belfast [PRONI]).

For 1641 and 1681 there are the *Books of Survey and Distribution* i.e. an English Government list of land ownership for distribution after confiscation. This material—from which the results from County Meath are lacking—is in NAI, with microfilm copies in NLI

Below: The start of the official pedigree of the O'Neills, housed at the Genealogical Office in Dublin.

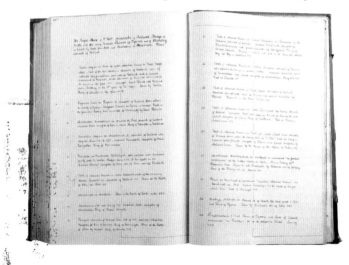

and transcripts in the Royal Irish Academy, Dublin (RIA). The books for Counties Roscommon, Mayo, Galway and Clare have been published by the Irish Manuscripts Commission (IMC). For 1641 to 1698, *Lists of Outlaws* consist of over 6,000 names of people outlawed whose lands were confiscated—microfilm copies of an abstract are in NLI.

For 1654, the *Civil Survey of Ireland* (published by IMC in 3 volumes in 1931), covers Counties Tipperary, Limerick, Waterford, Meath, Donegal and Derry, with incomplete entries for Counties Kerry, Dublin, Kildare, Wexford and Tyrone. It lists the landlords of each townland and their predecessors in 1641. For 1654, the *Down Survey* gives names of landowners and their religion (published by the Irish Archaeological Society in 1851). For 1659, there is a census of most counties, compiled by Sir William Petty (published by IMC in 1931, ed. Seamus Pender, *The Census of Ireland*).

Above: A page from the Book of the Boyles, with the various families represented heraldically.

For 1662 to 1666 Subsidy Rolls are principally concerned with Ulster. They list the nobility, clergy and laity who paid grants in aid to King Charles II. Some of these rolls are in NAI and PRONI, with transcripts in the Representative Church Body Library, Dublin (RCBL). For 1664 to 1666, Hearth Money Rolls give the name of each householder whose dwelling had a hearth. Copies of various of these are in GO, NAI, NLI, PRONI and RCBL.

For 1689 and 1690, information on Irish Jacobites is given by John D'Alton in *Illustrations Historical and Genealogical of King James II's Irish Army List* (published in 1689, and reissued in 1861); and in ed. C. E. Lart, *The Pedigrees and Papers of James Terry 1690–1725* (1938). For 1703, the Convert Rolls list Roman Catholics who changed their religion to the Church of

Ireland (published in IMC Reports in 1981, ed. Eileen O'Byrne). For 1740, there is a list of Protestant householders in several Ulster counties available in GO.

A large number of legal deeds, from 1708 onwards, are registered with indexes in the Registry of Deeds, Dublin (RD). Newspapers began in Ireland in the early 18th century. Good collections of them are held in NLI. Names and addresses of persons engaged in business are in the various directories which were published from the mid 18th century onwards. The best collections of these directories are in NAI and NLI.

Only people of substance made wills, but much information can be gleaned from them. A huge collection of wills, dating from 1536 to 1900, was destroyed in a fire in the Public Record Office of Ireland, Dublin (PROI) in 1922, but copies, abstracts, or indexes of over 60 per cent of them survive in NAI. There are also substantial holdings in GO, NLI and PRONI. Some of the material has been published in journals, and by Sir Arthur Vicars, *Index to the Prerogative Wills of Ireland 1536-1810* (Dublin, 1897).

There are fragments of Roman Catholic parish records dating from the late 17th century, but the first appreciable collections are much later —beginning variously in the later 18th century and the 19th century. They contain details of baptisms and of marriages. Microfilm copies of almost all this material are in NLI, but diocesan permission is required to consult some of it. Church of Ireland (Protestant) registers began earlier—some as early as the mid 17th century. Most of its parish registers up to 1871 were destroyed by

Below: Only people of substance made wills, but much information can be gleaned from them.

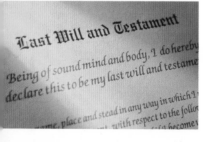

Last Will and Testament

Being of sound mind and body, I do hereby declare this to be my last will and testame

This Certificate is not available for purposes of Secondary Education.

CERTIFIED COPY of an ENTRY of BIRTH.

(Issued for the purposes of the Factory and Workshop Act, 1901.)

Registration District of *Greenwich*

Sub-District of *Deptford North* in the County of *London*

No.	When and where born	Name (if any)	Sex	Name and Surname of Father	Name and Maiden Surname of Mother	Rank or Profession of Father	Signature, Description, and Residence of Informant	When Registered	Signature
205	Thirty first October 1911 50. Blackhorse Road	Margaret Mary	girl	Thomas Kelly	Edith Maud Kelly formerly Bransbury	Bricklayer's Labourer	E. M. Kelly Mother 50 Blackhorse Road	Twelfth December 1911	M.

fire in the PROI in 1922, but RCBL—where the Church of Ireland archives are preserved—has worked admirably to restore the losses. Some records of Presbyterian congregations also date to the 17th century, but registers were not comprehensively undertaken until the 19th century. Microfilms of most of these registers from Northern Ireland until 1900 are in PRONI, whereas most from the rest of Ireland are in local custody. Copies of Methodist and Quaker records are also kept in PRONI. Good lists for clergymen of all denominations are on microfilm in NLI, some of them reaching back to the early 18th century.

For 1775–76, there is a list of Roman Catholics from various counties who took the Oath of Allegiance to the king of England (published in the *59th Report of the Deputy Keeper* of PROI). For 1778–93, Catholic Qualification Rolls list other Roman Catholics who took the Oath. An index to it—containing names, occupations, dates and places—survives in NAI.

Above: Birth certificates are housed at the General Register Office in Dublin.

Above: For 1796 a Spinning-Wheel Entitlement gives the names of persons who received spinning wheels as part of a government scheme.

For 1795, the Charter Trust Fund Marriage Certificates in NAI list Protestant labourers in north Leinster and County Cavan who were given small gratuities on marriage. For 1796, a Spinning Wheel Entitlement gives by district the names of persons—almost 60,000 in all, mostly in Ulster—who received free spinning wheels through a government scheme to encourage the linen trade. Indexes to the list are in NAI and PRONI. Details from two interesting local census survive—one from Elphin Diocese in 1749 (in NAI); and one for the town of Carrick-on-Suir in 1799 (microfilm copy in NLI).

For 1823 to 1838, the Tithe Applotment Books, and related material for all Ireland, specify the amount of money to be paid by each landholder to the Church of Ireland. Poor people also had to pay these tithes. The originals are in NAI; with microfilm copies in NLI and (for the nine Ulster counties) in PRONI. For 1848 to 1864, the Valuation of Ireland was carried out under the direction of Richard Griffith (published at the time by the General Valuation Office, Dublin [GVO], as *The Valuation of Ireland*). Householders' names are listed by county, barony, parish and townland. The surnames which occur in this source and in the Tithe Applotments are arranged by parish in a combined index, copies of which are in NLI, NAI, PRONI and GO. Less extensive revaluation books, covering the period down to 1929, are in GVO and PRONI. From 1837 to 1896, the

Below: Irish peasantry. Tithes fell most heavily on the poor.

Incumbered Estate Records, with details concerning the estates of bankrupt landlords, are preserved in NLI. For 1876, *Landowners in Ireland* (published officially in London in 1876) gives a list of the 32,614 persons—identified by province and county—who owned land exceeding an acre in that year.

Of great value are the National School Records for 1831 to 1921, which give the name, age and religion of each pupil, as well as the parents' address and occupation. PRONI has most of these registers for the six northern counties, but for the other 26 counties the school records are still kept locally. From 1838 to 1848, the Poor Law Records give details of inmates of workhouses and infirmaries—parts survive and are available in NAI, PRONI and county libraries. With the introduction of the Old Age Pension scheme in 1908, much information was assembled concerning the claimants and their families—these records are preserved in NAI and PRONI. Much more comprehensively, the General Register Office, Dublin (GRO) has

Below: Irish schoolgirls in the 1890s. National school records are of great value in tracing your genealogy.

Above: A 19th-century workhouse. Poor Law records can provide details of inmates of workhouses between 1838 and 1848.

Right: A cartoon satirising the policies which caused large numbers of people to emigrate from Ireland.

records of all births, marriages, and deaths, from 1864 for all counties up to 1921, and for the 26 counties of the Republic thereafter. For the six northern counties after 1921, these records are held in The Register General, Belfast (RG).

There are also other lists and valuations, variously kept in GO, NAI, NLI, PRONI, TCD and other locations. These include local lists of freeholders compiled from the 17th century onwards. From the same period are miscellaneous voters' lists and poll-tax books. More comprehensive are the lists of, and files on, state prisoners and convicted persons, covering the period 1788 to 1868, in the State Paper Office, Dublin (SPO). Militia and army lists from 1750 onwards are preserved variously in GO, NLI, PRONI and the Public Record Office at Kew in Surrey, England. Details of policemen for all of Ireland, from 1816 to 1922, are kept in microfiche copies in NAI and PRONI.

The most efficient method of tracing relatives would be from census reports; however, the material available is very unsatisfactory. A full census of Ireland was taken every ten years from 1821 to 1911, but only

Left: A sketch of a man taking a census around 1870. A full census of Ireland was taken every ten years from 1821 to 1911, but only fragments of these records remain.

fragments of these records remain. Now in NAI, they are as follows: 1821 (partially for Counties Cavan, Fermanagh, Galway, Meath and Offaly); 1831 (partially for County Derry); 1841 (Killeshandra in County Cavan only); 1851 (partial, mostly from County Antrim). In addition, some transcripts and abstracts made from the original 1841 to 1891 returns have been found. This means that the earliest comprehensive returns which survive come from the census taken in 1901 and 1911, kept in NAI. Copies of the 1901 returns for the six counties of Northern Ireland are also available at PRONI. No census was taken in 1921, and subsequent census are subject to a 100-year closure.

Derived from several of the above-mentioned sources is the Irish section of the *International Genealogical Index*, compiled by the Church of Jesus Christ of Latter-Day Saints (CLDS) and available in their major repositries. For detailed information on sources and how to consult them, see John Grenham, *Tracing Your Irish Ancestors* (Dublin, 1999).

THE DOYLES

SEANCHAS DÚLLACH

THIS WIDESPREAD SURNAME IS USED

BY MEMBERS OF DIFFERENT FAMILIES

IN IRELAND, THE VARIOUS

ANCESTORS OF WHOM WERE

CALLED DUBHGHALL OR BY A

SIMILAR-SOUNDING NAME. THE

MOTTO CLAIMED BY MANY OF THEM

IS, IN LATIN, *FORTITUDINE VINCIT* ('BY

FORTITUDE HE CONQUERS').

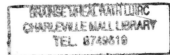

ORIGIN OF THE NAME

The name Dubhghall means 'dark-haired foreigner' and indicates Norse origin. As a patronymic, the son of a man with this name would be referred to as *mac Dubhghall*, and a grandson as *ua Dubhghaill*. Such designations came to be used in a general sense as surnames in mediaeval Ireland. Thus the surname Ua Dubhghaill was often adopted, and this in modernised spelling is Ó Dúill and anglicised as Doyle. Less widespread was the surname Mac Dubhghaill, which in modernised spelling is Mac Dúill, and is anglicised as MacDowell.

The Irish word *Gall* has a curious history. The Continental Celts were often referred to by the Greeks as 'Galati'. This was a native Celtic term for warriors, being based on the word *gal* ('ability' or 'valour'), and it was known in early Ireland also, for one of the constituent peoples of the ancient Laighin (Leinstermen) were known as Gaileoin or Gailing. There were groups of them in different parts of Ireland, but especially in the north midlands. Like other Celtic groups, they would have come originally from Britain, but their name might indicate that an earlier origin on the Continent was not forgotten by them.

The Romans tended to call the Celts by the term 'Galli', a corruption of 'Galati'. In the early centuries AD this came into increasingly wider usage to refer to the Celtic tribes, and their regions came to be called 'Gallia'. This (in English 'Gaul') was used especially in reference to their territories in modern-day France and adjacent areas. In or about the fourth century these terms were borrowed from Latin into the Irish

Left: Lough Tay in the Wicklow mountains. Doyle is a widespread surname in Ireland, and the second most common name in County Wicklow.

Above: Reconstruction of a Celtic settlement, near Quin, Co. Clare.

language. Thus the Latin singular Gallus in Irish became 'Gall', the Latin plural Galli became in Irish 'Gaill', and the collective territorial name Gallia became in Irish 'Gaille'.

There is indeed evidence for the presence of Gaulish mercenaries in Ireland in these centuries, particularly among the Laighin in the east of Ireland, and among the Déise in the south-east who were of ancient Érainn stock. For the Laighin, the Uí Gharrchon and the Uí Eineachghlais septs (in modern Counties Kildare and Wicklow), each had a family designated as Gaill; and for the Déise there were no less than three such families. All of these families bore the name of their own specific male progenitor, probably a mercenary.

The word used in Irish for a Celt from Britain was originally Cruithin, but by this time it had been displaced by another borrowing from Latin, Breatan. These were the strangers near at hand. Further away, the inhabitants of Gaul (by then largely Romanised) were considered to be more typically foreign, and therefore the word Gall gradually came to be used in the more general sense of 'foreigner'. When the Norsemen started to raid Ireland in the late eighth century, the term began to be used particularly of them.

Left: A first-century Celtic hammered bronze disc.

THE DANES OF THE CITIES

Right: A Viking raiding fleet. In the eighth century these Norsemen from Scandinavia arrived, plundering and looting the monasteries and treasures that lay close to the sea and rivers.

Below: Cattle graze near a stone structure at the ancient monastic centre of Clonmacnoise. Turgesius is reputed to have seized this site during the Norse raids of the eighth and ninth centuries.

The Norsemen who, with increasing ferocity, raided Ireland from 795 to 850 were mostly from Norway. The most successful of them was one Thorgils or 'Turgesius', who is reputed to have seized the great ecclesiastical centres of Armagh and Clonmacnoise and to have placed his fleets on Lough Neagh and on the rivers Boyne and Shannon. He was defeated and drowned in Lough Owel, on the Shannon,

in 845 by Maol Seachnaill, the high-king of Tara. Turgesius' practice of first raiding and then settling parts of the countryside was, however, a precedent followed by many of the other raiding Norse chiefs. Their pincipal settlements were at convenient harbours or river-mouths, where they built fortresses to be used as bases for further conquest. The most important of these bases were Dublin, Waterford and Limerick.

In or about the year 850 new groups of Norsemen began to arrive. These originated not in Norway but in Denmark, and the two groups of foreigners were soon in contention with each other. In order to distinguish them, the Irish referred to the Norwegians as Fionn-Ghaill ('fair-haired foreigners') and the Danes as Dubh-Ghaill ('dark-haired foreigners'). In 852, the Danes plundered Dublin, and then inflicted crushing defeats on the fleets associated with the Norwegian settlements at Annagassan and Carlingford (in modern County Louth). Soon after, another Danish fleet rounded the south-western coast of Ireland and sailed up the Shannon. They attacked the Norwegian settlement at Limerick, but did not succeed in taking it.

Above: Full-length view of the Cross of Scriptures at the religious site of Clonmacnoise.

Left: An excavation for Viking artifacts and footpaths takes place in Dublin.

In 853, two powerful Danish leaders, Olaf and Ivar, arrived in Dublin, which they took over. They then gradually extended their power over most of the Norsemen in Ireland. The Irish kings began to organise their forces in more skilful ways, however, and scored several victories against them—most notably when the high-king, Aodh Fionnliath, cleared the whole north coast of them in 866. In the south, the settlement at Youghal was destroyed by the Déise in the same year, and in the following years the Norsemen of Limerick, Waterford, and Wexford were defeated. Ivar died in 872, and in 902 his sons with their followers were driven out of Dublin itself. They went to join other Norsemen who had settled in the Western Isles of Scotland, in the Isle of Man, and in north-eastern England.

In the meantime, there was much intermarriage between the Norse and the Irish, especially in Leinster, at the level of the chieftains and also at the level of the ordinary populace. Many of the Norse were adopting Christianity, alliances between them and various native septs became common, and the Norse and the Irish borrowed names from each other. Hostilities again began in 914, when two grandsons of Ivar, Ragnall and Sigtrygg, retook Waterford. In 916 Sigtrygg recovered Dublin, and three years later he defeated and slew the high-king of Ireland, Niall 'black-knee' in the Dublin mountains. The Norse kingdom of Dublin was soon extended to cover much of the modern Counties Dublin and

Below: Viking swords discovered in Denmark.

Left: A modern-day view of the city of Waterford. The early fortified Viking city was confined to the small area between the river and what is now Christchurch Cathedral.

Wicklow. When, in 977, the able Dublin king, Olaf Kvaran, son of Sigtrygg, inflicted a major defeat on the high-king, Domhnall Ó Néill, the Norse overlordship was extended westwards as far as the Shannon.

The tide was soon to turn again, however. The high-king, Maol Seachnaill II, fought successful campaigns against the Dublin Norse from 979 to 1002, and in Munster the celebrated Brian Boru destroyed their kingdom at Limerick. When Brian took over the high-kingship, even Dublin fell to him; and when in 1014 Norse reinforcements came from abroad he defeated them at the Battle of Clontarf near Dublin. At the point of victory, the elderly Brian was attacked in his tent by the fleeing Danish leader, Brodir, and both fell in a titanic struggle.

The Norse population of the seaports did not

Below: The celebrated Munster high-king, Brian Boru.

Above: Brian Boru is killed after the Battle of Clontarf by the Danish leader, Brodir. Below: Loch Bracadale in the Scottish Hebrides.

immediately vanish after this battle, however, and indeed Dublin, Waterford, and Limerick continued to be largely Danish cities until the 13th century. Abroad, although York and their surrounding kingdom of the Danelaw was lost to them, the kingdoms in the Hebrides and the Isle of Man remained under the Norwegian and Danish settlers for several generations more. In these parts of the three Gaelic countries —Ireland, Scotland, and Man—a mixed population grew up who became known as Gall-Ghaeil ('foreigner Irish'). This general situation is in fact reflected by two significant placenames—Inse Gall ('the island of the foreigners') for the Hebrides, and Fine Gall ('the foreign clan') for the north of modern County Dublin.

DESIGNATION BECOMES A NAME

It was natural that a man of Danish, or partly Danish, stock would be known to his neighbours as Dubhghall, and there is no doubt that the grandchildren of several individuals so called took the surname Ua Dubhghaill. Since there are no quoted genealogies for the surname, these individual ancestors called Dubhghall cannot be clearly identified. Like the ancient sub-tribes of the Laighin and Déise, some individuals called 'Gall' may have owed their name to different foreign contacts or even to tribal tradition. It is, however, reasonable to assume that most bearers of the name originated in Danish settlements or in their hinterlands.

Bearers of the surname Doyle are most numerous in Leinster, and this can easily be related to the history of

Below: County Laois in the province of Leinster. Bearers of the Doyle surname are most numerous in Leinster.

Right: A Viking cargo ship or 'knarr'. Shorter and wider than the sleek longship, it was suited to carrying cargo such as cattle, wool, timber and wheat, for trading.

the Danish-controlled areas. Dublin was one of the most powerful cities in the Norse world, with dependent settlements further north along the coast in Carlingford and Strangford. Southwards, it controlled the whole coastal area as far as the settlements at Wicklow and Arklow. Most important was the immediate hinterland of Fine Gall—stretching to the Delvin river in the north and to Leixlip in the west—which was heavily settled with Norse traders and farmers. Furthermore, the rulers of Waterford and Wexford belonged to the same dynasty as the Dubliners, and were therefore closely allied with them. The Cork

Norsemen were also connected to the Danes of Dublin, but the large settlement at Limerick was largely Norwegian and followed its own independent course.

These vigorous coastal settlements specialised in overseas trade, for the Norsemen had established powerful centres across Europe extending all the way from Iceland in the west to the Black Sea in the east. Ireland thus owes much of its sea-going and economic traditions to the coastal settlements, and many words for these activities in the Irish language are borrowed from Norse. One mediaeval Irish poet described the Norsemen as notable for 'sailing the sea, huge appetites, and commerce'.

Eventually, the Norse language spoken in the settlements gave way to Irish but, considering their extensive influence on Irish life and the proliferation of the Gall-Ghaeil population, the nickname Dubhghall must have been frequent for individuals of Danish or partly Danish descent. The best-known personage referred to by this name was Dubhghall, brother of the Dublin

Below: The Battle of Clontarf where the Norse battalion commander known as Dubhghall was killed.

Above: New Ross in County Wexford. The Doyles of this area descend mainly from individuals with the name Dubhghall, the nickname for those of Danish descent. Below: The river Boyne. The Ciannachta inhabited Duleek on the banks of this river.

king, Sigtrygg 'silkenbeard', both being sons of Olaf Kvaran. He was a battalion commander who was slain in the Battle of Clontarf. The bridge over the river Liffey at Oxmantown in Dublin was called Droichead Dubhghaill, which indicates that it was built by a man known by that name. A place in Fine Gall, near to the coast, was called 'the town of Dubhghall', Baile Dubhghaill (now 'Baile Dhúill', anglicised as 'Baldoyle'); and an identical placename is found some

distance to the west of Fine Gall, at Kilmessan in County Meath.

Although there is little doubt that most of the Doyles native to Counties Dublin, Wicklow and Wexford are descended from individuals called by this name, it should also be noted that Dubhghall came into use as a personal name among the native Irish septs. For instance, in a region just to the north of Fine Gall, we find a local Irish chieftain bearing the name Dubhghall in the tenth century. He belonged to a section of the Ciannachta who inhabited the area of Duleek on the banks of the Boyne. These Ciannachta were of ancient Érainn origin, and they claimed that their eponymous ancestor, Cian, was a native of Munster. Cian's son, Tadhg, they said, had assisted the Connachta to gain control of the Boyne valley, and as reward got as much territory as he could circle in his chariot on one day. It may be that this Dubhghall of the Ciannachta was the ancestor of some of the Doyles of north Dublin and south Louth.

Another example is that of a king of the Ulstermen called Dubhghall, who reigned from 919 until his death at the hands of fellow Ulstermen in 925. He was the son of Aodh, who had preceded him in the kingship, and they belonged to the Dál Fiatach sept whose origins stretched back into prehistory as kings of the northern province. They had once controlled most of the north of Ireland, and from their ancient feats had developed the great epic stories of legendary Ulster heroes such as

Above: The Mourne mountains in County Down. The Doyles of this area may descend from Dubhghall, king of the Ulstermen of the Dál Fiatach sept.

Above: A sunset over Strangford Lough. There was a strong and influential Danish settlement at Strangford.

Conchobhar Mac Neasa and Cú Chulainn. In the fifth century AD, the Dál Fiatach were pushed eastwards from their ritual centre of Navan Fort (in County Armagh), and from then on their kingdom was confined to the area of modern County Down.

The genealogy of these Ulster kings is extant in the direct line from Muireadhach Muindearg at the beginning of the sixth century down to the end of the Middle Ages, when they gave rise to the Ulster families of MacGuinness, MacDunlevy, O'Haughey, MacArdle and MacCartan. The reason why their Dubhghall was so-called seems clear, for the strong and influential Danish settlement of Strangford was within the territory of the Ulstermen. After his death, his brother Matadán took over, and from this Matadán were descended the succeeding kings. The progeny of Dubhghall is unknown, but it is reasonable to consider some of the Doyles of the north-east as of that line.

The popularity of the name spread far to the west, where one Dubhghall was slain in 979. He was in fact a great-grandson of the high-king of Ireland, Aodh Fionnliath, and was the chieftain of Magh Íotha, the plain south of Derry city. After his death, his descendants upheld his prestige, perhaps giving rise to some instances of the surname in that area also. Yet another Dubhghall was father of Aodh, vice-abbot of the monastery of Clonfeacle on the Tyrone-Armagh border.

OTHER DOYLES

In County Roscommon was a family called Ó Dubhghaile or Clann Dubhghaile. The name was probably a corruption of Clann Duach-Ghalaigh, which would indicate that they were a branch of the well-known Clann Duach, descendants of Dauí Galach, king of Connacht from 482 to 502. His name meant Dauí 'of valour', and he was the son of Brion, brother of the famous Tara king, Niall. His descendants, the Clann Duach, were better known as the Uí Bhriúin, and they included many Connacht kings. In the Middle Ages, the families derived from these kings took on various surnames, becoming such as the O'Connors, O'Flahertys, O'Rourkes, and O'Reillys of later times. The Clann Dubhghaile from County Roscommon were thus of noble Irish lineage, who, because of the similarity in pronunciation ('o doo-le'), adapted their surname to the form Ó Dúill and anglicised it as Doyle. They should not be confused with the other, more numerous midland family called Ó Dubhlaoich, of Leinster stock who anglicise their name as 'Dooley'.

Some explanations for the adoption of the surname Doyle are more complicated—for instance in County Carlow and

Below: A grave slab commemorating Máelán mac Cathmhogha, king of the Uí Bhriúin of southern Connacht.

Above: County Carlow with the Blackstairs mountains in the background. In this county the Doyle surname derived from a chieftain by the name of Dubhghiolla (literally 'dark-haired servant'.

adjacent areas, where the surname Ó Dubhghiolla derived from a ninth century chieftain called Dubh-ghiolla. This chieftain belonged to an important line of the ancient Laighin who traced their ancestry to the mythical king Cathaoir, through his favourite son, Fiacha Baicidh. The historical Éanna Cinsealach, king of Leinster, was reputedly a great-grandson of Fiacha. Éanna, who flourished in the mid fifth century AD, was succeeded as king of the province by several of his descendants. One of the most important of these—although he did not actually become provincial king—was his great-grandson Cormac, whose progeny were known as Síol Chormaic.

Although they provided a few more provincial

kings, this Síol Chormaic gradually lost their promi-
nence and were much reduced by the late eighth century. At that time, a branch of them was led by one
Aodh, son of Cairbre, who gained a new territory in the
centre of Leinster. This had previously belonged to far-
out relatives of his, the progeny of Drón, brother of
Éanna Cinsealach. The kingdom was therefore called Uí
Dhróna, and is the area covered by the two baronies
called in English 'Idrone', which form the western part
of modern County Carlow.

Aodh's son and successor was called Bruadar, a
name not uncommon in Ireland at the time, being a
borrowing of the Welsh word for a 'dream'. Dubhghiolla
was the son of this Bruadar, and he became lord of
Idrone in 851. Some of his sons were slain in 893, but
one of those who survived was Rian, ancestor of the
Ryan family of Leinster. The descendants of other sons
of Dubhghiolla took their surname directly from him.
This would have been Ó Dubhghiolla (literally 'grandson of Dubhghiolla'), pronounced 'o duv-yilu', but
through changes in the spoken language in the Middle
Ages its pronunciation developed into 'o doo-lu'.

A common way of referring to a family in Irish is to
use a group form of the surname, such as in the case of
Dubhghiollaigh. In post-mediaeval Leinster, this was
pronounced 'doo-lu', identical with the pronunciation
of Dubhghallaigh ('Doyles'). The ancestor's name was
thus taken to have been Dubhghall, a misinterpretation
strengthened by his father's name, Bruadar, being considered a variant of the Danish 'Brodir' (literally
'brother'). Thus this native Leinster family was considered to be of Danish origin and its surname was adapted
to Ó Dúill and anglicised as Doyle.

Similar misinterpretations may have given rise to

Above: The Beare Peninsula on the border of Counties Cork and Kerry. As in several other areas, the origins of the Doyles in these counties may be Irish rather than Norse.

the surname in a few other cases also. For instance, among the Uí Chinsealaigh, the strong Wexford sept who also descended from Éanna Cinsealach, there was in the mid tenth century a chieftain named Bruadar, whose father was called Dubhghiolla. Neither is it clear whether the Doyles of Counties Cork and Kerry derive from some Norseman of Cork called Dubhghall or from a Dubhghiolla, which name was also found among the ancient Érainn sept called Múscraighe in west Munster.

THE MACDOWELLS

I n the wars from the 13th to the 16th century, the Irish chieftains often hired mercenaries from the western islands of Scotland. Inse Gall was the term used for these Hebridean islands because of the strong Norse settlements there, and thus the mercenaries were known in Irish as *Gallóglaigh* ('foreign volunteers'). A number of Irish families are of the stock of these fighters—such as the MacSweeneys, Sheehys, MacAlisters, and Galloglys.

Also included among them are the MacDowells, whose surname in the singular is simply Mac Dubhghaill ('son of the dark-haired foreigner'). They were definitely of Norse-Gaelic origin in the southern Hebrides, being descended from a chieftain called Dubhghall, who ruled over the islands of Jura, Tiree, Coll and Mull in the later 12th century. He was son of Somerled (d.1164), and his brother, Randal, ruled over Islay, Kintyre, and Arran. From this Randal, in fact, was descended the most powerful family of the Hebrides in later times, the MacDonalds.

Above: The peaks of hills around Loch Scridain on the island of Mull, Scotland. The MacDowells are descended from a chieftain called Dubhghall who ruled over Mull along with Jura, Coll and Tiree in the later 12th century.

Right: The MacDonald tartan. The MacDonald family were one of the most powerful families in the Hebrides in later times.

The western coast of Scotland had, of course, been settled from Ireland long before and, despite his Norse name, Somerled was largely of Irish descent. The genealogists traced his origins to Fearghus Mac Earca, a king of Dál Riada who led the Irish settlements on the Scottish coast in the late fifth century, and this would appear to have some basis. A long tradition of historiography and a shared Gaelic language kept alive a shared sentiment between Scotland and Ireland and, when they returned as mercenaries, the MacDowells (alias MacDougalls) did not really regard themselves as the foreigners which their name implied. They settled in different parts of Ulster, where the surname is still numerous; and also in the area around Roscommon town, where the placename Lios Mhac Dúill (anglicised as Lismacdowell) commemorates them.

THE DOYLES IN RECENT CENTURIES

In recent centuries Doyles have been to the fore in various fields of endeavour. Several of them have become prominent public figures. James Warren Doyle (1786–1834) was training for the priesthood in Portugal when the Peninsula wars disrupted his studies in 1806. He served as an interpreter for the army of Sir Arthur Wellesley (later the duke of Wellington). In later life he became the bishop of Kildare and Leighlin (1819). In this position he became involved in the social struggles of the laity, openly supported Daniel O'Connell and was a fierce critic of the British administration. The bishop also worked to build libraries and schools in his diocese.

Sir John Doyle (1756–1834), born in Dublin, reached the rank of general in the British army and raised the 87th Regiment (Royal Irish Fusiliers). He also served as private secretary to the Prince of Wales (who was later crowned King George IV), was elected MP for Mullingar in 1783, and became governor of Guernsey.

Ephraim McDowell (1771–1830) was the grandson of an Irish Protestant who emigrated to the United States. McDowell practiced surgery and was a pioneer in abdominal surgical techniques, performing the first

Below: Irish politician and activist Daniel O'Connell who championed the cause of Irish Catholics. James Warren Doyle, bishop of Kildare and Leighlin, openly supported him.

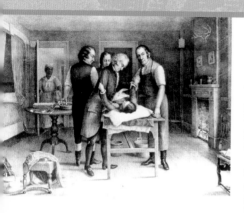

Above: The surgeon Ephraim McDowell performing the first ovariotomy in America.

ovariotomy in the United States in 1809. One of his most famous patients was James K. Polk, for whom he removed a gall stone and repaired a hernia. He was also well known for his generosity, and he performed considerable work for charity.

Sarah Doyle (1830–1922) is best remembered as an American feminist and educator. She was a driving force behind the foundation of Brown's Women's College and the construction of its first building, Pembroke Hall (1887). The building marked a change in the education of women.

Various Doyles and McDowells have found fame in the arts and media. The artist John Doyle (1797–1868), born in Dublin, left for London in 1821 where he hoped to establish himself as a portrait painter. He failed to sell enough pictures but became a talented lithographer. He revolutionised the art of caricature and his pictures appeared in *The Times*. His son, Richard, also became a cartoonist; and his other son, Charles—who went to live in Scotland—was the father of the writer Arthur Conan Doyle.

The cartoonist Richard Doyle (1824–) began having his work published at the age of 15. By 1848 he was producing a third of the cartoons that appeared in the satirical magazine *Punch*. The famous *Punch* cover used by the magazine between 1849 and 1956 was designed by him.

The Scottish writer and medical doctor Sir Arthur Conan Doyle (1859–1930) is best known for his creation of the detective Sherlock Holmes. The fictional detective is one of the most vivid and enduring characters of English fiction. Holmes first appeared in 'A Study in Scarlet' in *Beeton's Annual* of 1887.

US composer Edward A. MacDowell (1860–1908) held the first chair of music at Columbia University (1896–1904). His outstanding works are four piano sonatas: *Tragica* (1893), *Eroica* (1895), *Norse* (1900) and *Keltic* (1901). His *Indian Suite* (1897) for orchestra employs adaptations of American Indian melodies. Smaller works include the popular *Woodland Sketches* (1896) and *Sea Pieces* (1898) for piano. His widow, Marian Nevins MacDowell, founded

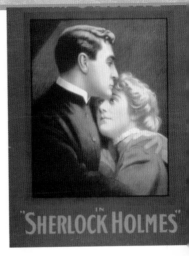

Above: A theatre poster for a production of *Sherlock Holmes*, featuring the famous detective character of that name created by Arthur Conan Doyle.

Left: A cartoon of a cricket match at Lords from *Mr Pips His Diary—Manners and Customs of Ye Englyshe in 1849* by Richard Doyle.

Right: The American composer Edward MacDowell.

The MacDowell Colony for artists at their summer home in 1907. Nearly 4,500 writers, visual artists, composers and film makers have used the New Hampshire colony studios. Some of the well known works created there include Leonard Bernstein's *Mass* and Aaron Copeland's *Appalachian Spring*.

Lynn C. Doyle ('linseed oil') is the pseudonym of the writer Leslie A. Montgomery (1873–1961) who was born in County Down. He wrote over 20 books, including the humourous Ballygullion series about a fictional border village. His first novel, *Mr Wildridge at the Bank* (1916), was followed by a succession of short stories, poems and plays.

Stuart Doyle (1887–1945) had a major role in developing Australia's motion picture industry. He founded the Australian Broadcasting Company to provide a national wireless service. It was taken over by the federal government (1932) and became the Australian Broadcasting Commission. He went on to establish cinema chains and film production companies.

The English actor Roddy McDowall (1928–98) starred as a child with Elizabeth Taylor in *Lassie Come Home* (1943) and films such as *How Green Was My Valley* (1941). He went on to star in several acclaimed motion pictures, including *Cleopatra* (1963) and *Planet of the Apes* (1968), in which he played Cornelius, the ape. McDowall, who was also a respected photographer, enjoyed capturing other celebrities on film, and some of his work can be seen in his books such as *Double Exposure* (1966).

English actor Malcolm McDowell (real name Taylor) changed his name to his mother's maiden name because there was another actor in England named

Left: The English actor Roddy McDowall starred in several acclaimed films.

Malcolm Taylor. His first motion picture was *Poor Cow* (1967). His scenes were subsequently cut, but he attracted the attention of director Lindsay Anderson, who cast the 25-year-old actor as a prep-school rebel in *If...* (1968). Director Stanley Kubrick was likewise impressed by McDowell's ability to project working class insolence; Kubrick starred the actor as futuristic street gang leader Alex in *A Clockwork Orange* (1971). He subsequently starred in a number of hit motion pictures, including *Time After Time* (1979).

Above: The English actor Malcolm McDowell in costume on a film set.

The US actress Andie MacDowell (1958–) worked as a model and made her acting debut in *Greystoke: The Legend of Tarzan, Lord of the Apes* (1984). She has since had many opportunities to display her acting talent.

The Scottish film composer Patrick Doyle (1953–)

Right: Model-turned-actress Andie MacDowell as Jane in the film *Greystoke: The Legend of Tarzan, Lord of the Apes.*

Far left: The Scottish film composer Patrick Doyle.

Left: The author Roddy Doyle who won the Booker Prize for *Paddy Clarke Ha Ha Ha*.

is best known for his collaborations with actor/director Kenneth Branagh. He has composed film scores for *Much Ado about Nothing*, *Hamlet*, *Sense and Sensibility*, *Great Expectations* and *Bridget Jones' Diary*.

The novelist Roddy Doyle (1958–), born in Dublin, originally wrote satirical plays for Dublin's Passion Machine Theatre company. His popular novels include *The Commitments* (1987) and *Paddy Clarke Ha Ha Ha*, for which he won the 1993 Booker prize. He has also written scripts for films based on his works.

The Doyles and MacDowells have various military and naval connections. The American general Irvin McDowell (1818–85) was born in Ohio, but went to school in France and later graduated from West Point. McDowell is remembered for leading the losing Union forces in the First Battle of Bull Run (1861). Later he was in charge of the army which defended Washington D.C. He was also a leader in the Second Battle of Bull Run, and many people criticised his actions. After the

Above: The US general Irvin McDowell is remembered for leading the losing Union forces in the First Battle of Bull Run.

Below: The First Battle of Bull Run in 1861.

war, he continued to serve in the army until he retired in 1882. Later he moved to California and was the Park Commissioner of San Francisco. Another US commander was Major General Alexander McDowell McCook (1831–1903) who was appointed colonel of the First Ohio Volunteer Infantry in 1861, and commanded them at Bull Run. He was later cited for gallant and meritorious service at Nashville, Shiloh and Perryville. His reputation, however, was tarnished after his involvement at the Battle of Chickamauga (1863). McCook Nebraska is named after Alexander.

Company Sergeant Major Martin Doyle received Britain's Victoria Cross for gallantry on the Western Front in 1918. He later served as an IRA intelligence officer in the Anglo-Irish War (1919–22) and served in the army of the Irish Free State.

Carribbean nurse Mabel K. Doyle (1890–1989)

Left: The baseball player Larry Doyle practising pitching.

(married name Staupers) was responsible for eliminating segregation in the US Armed Forces Nurse Corps during the Second World War. She enlisted the support of First Lady Eleanor Roosevelt and initiated a national letter writing campaign to ensure black nurses were wholly accepted by 1945.

Several sporting heroes bear the name. Larry Doyle (1886–1974) began his US Major League baseball career in 1907 with the New York Giants. The 21-year-old went on to play for 14 seasons on two different teams and ended his big league playing career in 1920. Doyle led the National League with 172 hits in 1909, and batted a high of .330 in 1912. He won the National League batting title in 1915 with a .320 mark and league highs of 189 hits and 40 doubles. He stole 297 career bases, swiping home 17 times. He became a five-time .300 hitter.

Jack Doyle (1913–78), born in County Cork, became a champion boxer in Britain and his right-hand punch became notorious. He moved to the United

Above: The Irish boxer Jack Doyle was notorious for his right-hand punch.

States where he had a brief marriage to the Hollywood actress Judith Allen. After marrying Mexican starlet Movita they returned to Britain and became a singing act. Movita divorced him in 1945 to marry Marlon Brando. He took up all-in wrestling and drew great crowds, but eventually died in poverty.

The County Tipperary hurler, John Doyle (1930–), from Holycross, won eight All-Ireland Senior Hurling Championship medals over a period from 1949 to 1965. He also won a record 11 National League medals. The brilliant forward Jimmy Doyle (1937–), from Thurles, was one of his colleagues on the Tipperary team from 1958 onwards.

Mick 'Doyler' Doyle (1940–), born in County Kerry, played rugby for Garryowen, Blackrock College, University College Dublin, Cambridge University and Edinburgh Wanderers. He won 20 consecutive Ireland caps as a flanker (1965–68), three of them with his younger brother, Tommy, on the other flank. He later became a successful Leinster and national coach.

British footballer Mike Doyle (1946–) played in midfield and defence for Manchester City (1964–78). He originally joined as a member of the ground staff but was determined to play on the pitch he helped maintain. By 1975 he had been made team captain.

Several places bear the name. There are at least four occurrences in the south of Ireland of the placename Baile Uí Dhúill (anglicised as Ballydoyle), which indicates a townland belonging to a family called Doyle. The Ballydoyle in south Wexford is likely to refer directly to a family of Danish or partly Danish origin; but the places known by that name in the north of County Cork and in the south of County Tipperary are too far inland for such an interpretation, and may rather echo the presence of a family with that surname in more recent centuries. The same can be said of the placename Baile Uí Dhúill in north Kilkenny, which has been anglicised slightly differently as Ballydowel.

Further afield in the USA, Doylestown is a small village in Wayne County, Ohio. Another village of the same name is found in Columbia County, Wisconsin. Doylestown Borough can be found in Pennsylvania.

Today the Doyles, whose origins lie in Ireland, are to be found wherever Irish migrants have settled. While they have an ancient ancestry and noble lineage, they also play a major part in many areas of human endeavour across the globe.

Above: The footballer Mike Doyle made over 500 appearances for Manchester City.

Below: An aerial view of Doylestown Borough in Pennsylvania, USA.

Page numbers in *italic* refer to illustrations

PICTURE CREDITS

The publishers are grateful to the individual photographers and institutions who have made illustrations available for this book, as follows:

The Art Archive: 32, 36, 40

Chrysalis Books Archive: 6, 8, 9 (top), 9 (bottom), 11, 15 (top), 15 (bottom), 16, 20, 21, 24 (top), 24 (bottom), 28, 30, 35 (top), 39, 43, 45, 46, 48, 49, 50 (bottom)

Corbis: 1, 2, 13 (top), 13 (bottom), 14, 18, 19 (top), 19 (bottom), 22, 25, 33, 34 (bottom), 35 (bottom), 37, 38 (top), 38 (bottom), 41, 42 (top), 42 (bottom), 44, 50 (top), 53 (top), 54, 55, 58 (bottom), 59, 61 (bottom)

Mary Evans Picture Library: 10, 26 (top), 34 (top)

Hulton|Archive: 12, 26 (bottom), 27, 51, 52, 53 (bottom), 56 (top), 56 (bottom), 58 (top), 60, 61 (top)

Rex Features: 57 (left), 57 (right)

Antony Shaw: 23